HOW TO WIN IN COURT

Philip Gegan

Third Edition (May 2022)

To my darling wife Ruth

"Justice? You get justice in the next world. In this world you have the law."

William Gaddis

"Remember that it is not the lawyer who knows the most law, but the one who best prepares his case, who wins."

Napoleon Hill

"A jury consists of twelve persons chosen to decide who has the better lawyer."

Robert Frost

I have a few other books published on Amazon, and you can sample them by going to
https://www.amazon.com/Philip-Gegan/e/B01IBNHK00/

Disclaimer

While I have made every effort to supply valid, accurate information, no warranty is given that anything in this Guide is fit for purpose. I assume no liability or responsibility for errors, omissions or the way you interpret the contents or act upon them.

I do not intend this Guide to be a source of legal, accounting or business advice. You are advised to seek your own such advice as you think fit to suit your own individual circumstances. All the contents are subject to whatever local laws and regulations apply in the area where you live and operate.

The Purchaser or Reader of this publication assumes responsibility for the use of these materials and information. The Author and Publisher do not warrant the performance or

---

The image used on the front cover of this book is from an image supplied by Pixabay.

Table of Contents

Introduction to the Third Edition

During my years of practising law I found myself frequently advising clients about evidence. Many people find it difficult to grasp how vitally important it is to collect all the evidence you possibly can that may assist you in proving your case when court proceedings loom.

Often it was difficult to get the point across with sufficient emphasis. Sometimes I felt that I could have done with a wooden mallet to bash the client's head with as I underlined each syllable.

"It's all about the evidence."

"You—MUST—coll--ect--all--your--*ev--i--dence*!"

Court cases are largely decided on the *evidence*.

The evidence, *and the way in which it is*

presented.

Please remember that above all else when you're reading this Guide.

Phew! Here endeth the first lesson! Just a couple more things, and we'll begin.

First off, I refer to third parties, eg the other side's lawyer, in the masculine singular. Of course the other side's lawyer, and anyone else mentioned in this Guide, is just as likely to be female and/or plural. But for reasons of brevity I use "he" rather than "he or she" or "he, she or they". Besides, in England, under the *Interpretation Act* of 1888, in legal documents and statutes, etc, the singular is deemed to include the plural and the masculine is deemed to include the feminine. Okay, this book isn't a legal document, but this practice still sounds sensible to me.

The third edition has seen this Guide undergo a major rearrangement. Several appendices are now Sections in their own right. I have also strived to make this Guide more user-friendly throughout.

Enjoy your read. Oh, and did I mention? It's all about the EVIDENCE.

Philip Gegan

May 2022

Introduction to the First Edition

This is the advice your lawyer probably doesn't have the time to give you.

This Guide is not intended to be legal advice. Rather it is practical, down-to-earth guidance that supplements legal advice, and that applies in countries whose legal system is based on common law. Those countries include the UK, USA, Canada, Australia, New Zealand, and South Africa, as well as several other smaller countries, usually former territories that at one time were part of the British Empire.

My own background is as a lawyer in England, and in many parts of this Guide I have assumed that the law where you live is broadly similar. However, there may be differences, and of course there are always changes made in the law from time to time in all jurisdictions, and for those reasons you are advised to always seek local legal advice if you find yourself in any situation covered here.

I have written this primarily from the viewpoint of an *accused* in a criminal case or the *defendant* in a civil case. But if you are the *plaintiff* in a civil case then there is still plenty for you here, such as how to prepare your case and conduct yourself in court. In addition, the *Appendix -- How To Recover Money Owing To You (Including Draft Letters)* is written for the benefit of civil plaintiffs, or those who are at risk of having to sue.

I have not covered personal injuries litigation specifically, even though this is a very large and growing area of legal practice, because what I say in the Guide covers it in general terms, which is all that is possible in a Guide like this.

1. You Have A Problem

1. The Warning Light

If you're reading this you've already reached this stage of the proceedings. That's the red light that comes on in your mind when you <u>know</u> you have a problem. It may have been an argument with your neighbour or spouse, a road accident, or something that happened at work.

The realisation may be sudden or gradual, but at some point you'll know that you're facing potential or actual litigation. If there's one thing you need to know about litigation, it's this. You need to be on the winning side. This short Guide is designed to help you do just that.

2. It's All About Evidence

Court cases are won and lost on the evidence and the way it's put across.

That's not to say the party with the strongest

evidence will win the case, necessarily. Often the way it's presented, or how one or other of the parties or their lawyers appears to the judge or jury, will have a decisive effect. But nevertheless, evidence is vital.

This is seldom appreciated by non-lawyers until they find themselves caught up in court proceedings. Too much good evidence is lost and never made use of simply because the person who could have made use of it didn't realise at the time how vital it was.

If you don't have enough good evidence then you will find it difficult to impossible to win your case.

This short Guide will help you make sure that doesn't happen to you. So the first lesson here is how to collect and preserve your evidence -- all of it.

First things first -- what is "evidence"?

Evidence is a collection of facts relevant to your case, admissible to a court or tribunal. Under the law of most countries it is divided into three kinds --

(a) oral evidence,

(b) documentary evidence, and
(c) exhibits.

You have to collect all such evidence or facts that you can later present as evidence that will help you win in court, into whatever category it may fall. Let's take them one by one.

(a) Oral Evidence

Oral evidence is evidence given in court by a witness in answer to questioning. In exceptional cases a written statement can be admitted in evidence where, e.g., the witness is prevented by illness or frailty from attending the court hearing. All legal jurisdictions have their own rules on this. Written statements are of limited value, because they cannot be cross-examined (see below). In England, our system of justice is based on bringing out evidence in court by examination and cross-examination. This is covered in more detail in *Section 3 -- Winning In Court.*

A sub-category of oral evidence is *expert evidence*. This is evidence given by someone who is a recognized expert in a subject relevant to the points in issue in the case. he expert may be, for example, an insurance assessor, a surgeon, a soil analyst, or anyone with specialist knowledge of and experience in matters relevant to your case. Usually it is given in person at court, although it can be given as a report signed by the expert if attendance at court is impractical. Such evidence is normally accepted by both sides, though the opposing side can still cross-examine in order to clarify any points that may be to their favour.

(b) Documentary Evidence

Documentary evidence is anything presented to the court in written or printed form.

Do you have any documents, including official documents, that may help your case or avoid delays, e.g. marriage certificate, contract of employment, share certificate? What about letters written by your adversary? Even notes, drawings and diagrams are frequently produced in support of a lawsuit, so even if it doesn't seem to have any significance now, keep it. It may be worth its weight in gold later on.

Any correspondence you receive should be date-stamped the moment it arrives. Keep the envelope it arrived in and check the date stamped on it. Remember, these things might not seem important now, but they may be crucial later on. Keep all correspondence in a file and keep it in date order.

Adopt a business-like attitude to it, and that includes making notes of all telephone conversations as soon as they are complete.

Unless it's something that isn't very important, photograph or scan all such documents the day you receive them, so the date is recorded when you upload them to your computer (or the cloud) the same day. Again, back up these copies at regular intervals and keep a spare set online (password protected, of course). There are plenty of places that offer free online storage facilities, and probably your broadband supplier makes this available as part of your package.

This brings us to the role of technology in modern documentary evidence. With the increasing use of digital technology, electronic (or digital) evidence is becoming more commonplace. The law of evidence (which was complicated enough already), wherever you are, has thus become that much more complicated. If this affects you then you'll have to seek the advice of your lawyer, who may himself need specialist advice, according to the circumstances.

One good thing about modern digital technology, however, is that these days nearly everyone has with them nearly all the time a smartphone that can take photographs and/or video recordings. This capability can be invaluable, for example, in collecting evidence relating to a road accident, an assault by your spouse, and so on. The possibilities, as they say, are endless.

(c) Exhibits

Exhibits are things, e.g. a weapon used in a murder, a breathalyzer used in a drink-driving case. It can also include forensic evidence, e.g. fingerprints, a DNA sample.

Are there any items that may assist your case in any way? For example, a breathalyzer in a drink-driving charge, a knife used in a domestic violence incident by your spouse. If you can, collect such items and put them in a safe place. The breathalyzer in this example will be retained by the traffic police, so if you wish to question its accuracy or raise the question of when it was last calibrated, notify the authorities in writing that you may wish the instrument to be produced in court or made available for an independent test or analysis. And keep a copy of your letter. All such correspondence should be dated and either hand delivered by you or sent by recorded or registered post, or whatever means of delivery operating where you live whereby delivery can be proved.

If the item is in your possession keep it in a safe place, and if it may be forensically examined, e.g. for fingerprints or DNA, then take care not to contaminate it, e.g. wear gloves when handling it and don't handle it more often than absolutely necessary. Place with it a note of the date and time, and where it was found, plus evidence of this (see below) and the place where you're keeping it. It goes without saying that the place of safekeeping should be safe from any adversary, e.g. spouse, business partner.

Your smartphone or camera can probably time and date-stamp photographs. Get a date-stamped photograph or video clip of yourself holding the items. Keep these on your computer or smartphone, and make back-up copies to upload to a secure place online. If the original is lost or stolen you'll have a back-up somewhere where no-one can steal or destroy it.

3. More About Evidence That Your Lawyer Probably Doesn't Have Time To Tell You

Most court cases are won and lost before they ever reach court. They're won by the person who collects and preserves their evidence and prepares their case the more thoroughly.

Much of your case will consist of the evidence you give in court. If you are to win your case then you have to start by gathering your evidence at the earliest opportunity. If you are by nature a hoarder, and if you keep a diary, then the next part of the proceedings will not be burdensome to you. And if neither applies to you then, even so, it's not difficult. Let me explain.

As soon as you know you have a problem that could conceivably lead to court or tribunal proceedings, you MUST start keeping a written log of all occurrences to do with it. Even just a small notebook with a few notes jotted down from time to time can easily make all the difference between success and failure.

If you don't write notes at the time of the incident you'll forget it.

You won't be able to recall, later on in your lawyer's office or in court, even when it took place. You'll forget all the little details that will make your evidence convincing. So you MUST keep a journal as soon as you know you have a problem that could just end up in court.

But remember this. Your journal or notebook, if you refer to it in giving your evidence, is a "discoverable document", i.e. it can be examined by the lawyer on the other side. He will use it against you in whatever way he can. For example, he will suggest, if he can, that it is a fraudulent document containing a tissue of lies that you've invented about his client (your adversary), written by you some time after the incident it purports to describe.

You have to counter all such suggestions from the start. Before each entry, write the date and time that you're writing it. Write it as soon as you can after each incident (if you're at work, be careful about writing it in your employer's time - you'll be the best judge of that). You want things fresh in your mind when you put them down on paper.

If you type your notes on your computer or into your smartphone then the date should be automatically recorded as part of the file. If this is how you operate make sure that your potential adversary cannot gain access to your PC or phone.

In any event (and I know I've said this already but it's so important I'm saying it again), always upload your file to a secure server online, or keep back-up copies on a CD-ROM or memory stick, or, better still, make your files password-protected.

Anything, as long as there's no danger of your notes being destroyed without a back-up copy still being available to you somewhere.

Is the date and time stamp provided by your computer or smartphone software sufficient to prove the time you wrote the note? It should be, but nevertheless, at the same time as you write your account of an incident, put a note that will verify the actual date and time. This could be a note of the news headlines for that day, the winning lottery numbers, or what the weather was like, especially if it was unusual. Put this among your notes so that it can be verified later if in dispute that it was written at the time you say it was written. Don't leave anything to chance. People who do that lose in court.

Don't write anything in your notes that you wouldn't mind being read out in court. So any gratuitous insults and derogatory adjectives should be toned down. Write objectively as far as possible, as if you were a reporter on a local paper (but without any undue dramatization). Yes, it might be more boring, but that's how it should be done.

Remember to recount all relevant details, especially of words spoken. Often individuals have certain favourite expressions of speech and if you can record such an expression from your adversary in the context of what he said at the time then it will make your account of the event much more credible.

Add to your journal, or diary of events, on each relevant occasion. If it is your neighbour giving you trouble or your boss trying to manufacture an excuse to sack you, there are likely to be a number of times when words are exchanged. Make your notes on each occasion. Don't even hint to him that you're keeping a record.

Your account of each incident should reveal when and where it took place, what caused it (as far as you're able to say) and who was present. It's vital that you write down all relevant details, but be concise as far as possible. That is, don't put in unnecessary, irrelevant detail. Remember that your lawyer may be reading it before long, and after him your adversary's lawyer, and perhaps the judge and jury as well. So although you're writing these notes for yourself to assist your case, write them convincingly enough to destroy the other side.

Write an account of your case to give your lawyer at your first meeting. Don't make it too long. Cut out as much "opinion evidence" as you can. Keep it strictly to the point, addressing the issues at stake, e.g. your vehicle's make and model if you're charged with a driving offence. Set out what was said at important stages, and by whom. Give details where relevant, e.g. type of clothing worn by a witness, if his breath smelt of alcohol, and so on.

In a criminal case this written account will prove to be of great value to your lawyer in preparing your Defence Statement. In most legal jurisdictions this document is required by law to be filed at court, with a copy to the prosecution, within strict time limits. It sets out the nature of your defence, including any particular defences on which you intend to rely, and indicates any points of law that you wish to make, including any points as to the admissibility of evidence or abuse of process.

Your lawyer will explain more about this when the time comes, but the main point here is that your written notes will be a great help at this stage. The more meticulous your preparation, the greater your chances of winning in court.

As I said at the end of the section on Documentary Evidence (2(b) above), these days, with smartphones being so widely owned, it's much easier to take photographs of the scene of an incident. You may be able to capture witnesses in your photographs or video footage, but be cautious -- in some circumstances some people may object if they think you're photographing or filming them.

In many western countries, and certainly in the UK, CCTV is used extensively to monitor streets and road junctions, so many crimes and road accidents are actually filmed in this way. You're in the hands of the authorities if you wish to make use of any such evidence, so don't let this stop you from gathering your own as far as possible.

4. Looking After Your Witnesses

Some witnesses may be already known to you as, e.g., friends or work colleagues. In this case you should be able to continue your relationship as such without any problem. If any are strangers to you, then you should, as courteously and quickly as possible, collect their names and addresses. Of course, some may be unwilling to give you this information, which is understandable. In that case remain courteous and polite (remember, you may be relying on these people later on to help you win your case).

Perhaps they would be prepared to give you their email address, mobile phone number, or Twitter or Facebook ID (though this would be far less reliable than a postal address). Note their descriptions -- age, sex, demeanour, the clothes they were wearing -- and any distinguishing marks. It's often possible to trace witnesses later on from an accurate description noted at the time.

If you can, try and find out a little about them. Explain that if there are any court proceedings resulting from the incident, then you'd like them to be prepared to testify for you. Most people will agree to this, especially if such proceedings are far from certain. That will give you the opening you need to request their contact details.

As you speak with each potential witness, try to assess them and whether they would be likely to be of help with your case. Once you know them a little, check with them if they have any criminal convictions. This may have to be done tactfully, but it's important to know if they do have any, even if they occurred years ago. It can be very embarrasing in court, with one of your witnesses in the box, to have the opposing lawyer stand up and flourish a long list, saying, "Well, Mr Smith, it seems you're not entirely a stranger to the criminal courts!"

One final point here. <u>Keep in touch with your witnesses.</u> You don't want them moving away and not leaving you their forwarding address or phone number. Even mobile phone numbers frequently change. You could consider forming a Facebook group consisting of your witnesses (just to keep in touch, and not to exchange any messages that may prejudice your case -- remember that anything you put in an email message or on a Facebook message board, etc, is potentially viewable by millions of people).

I'm not saying you should be especially friendly with them, as sometimes this could go against you in court. But the occasional courtesy phone call, just so you can satisfy yourself they're still around and prepared to testify, doesn't go amiss. You can't rely completely on your lawyer for this.

5. What If The Problem Goes Away?

Unless you're completely satisfied it won't come back, e.g. the potential opposing party has died or emigrated, then keep your written notes, photographs, video and everything else.

Don't discard them just because things go quiet for a while. If you want to prove that your spouse has behaved violently, or your boss unreasonably, or your neighbour unneighbourly, then the further back your written notes and other recordings go, the better.

2. Preparing To Win - Getting the Right Legal Advice and Representation

1. Choosing A Lawyer

There have been litigants and defendants who've "gone it alone" and won, but it's very difficult. Judges tend not to favour those who represent themselves because all too often they have to be pulled up for breaching points of procedure, rules of evidence, and so on, and that wastes time and taxes their patience.

Here I'm assuming you intend to instruct a lawyer to represent you in court. If you don't then read this section anyway as it contains useful information that you'll need. See Section 7 for where you're acting for yourself without a lawyer.

2. Who To Instruct?

The first point, overlooked by many, is that you don't have to stick with the first lawyer you consult. If you sense after a while that he's not really interested in your case, not committed to getting the best result, or not quite up to the task, then look around for a replacement straight away.

Many lawyers these days operate on a "no win no fee" basis, so you'll have to be careful. A lawyer has a lien over his client's documents until his fees have been paid, i.e. he doesn't have to pass them to you or anyone else until he's been paid for his services to date.

If your legal fees are covered by insurance or legal aid then this shouldn't be a problem. If you're worried about this aspect, though, then keep a copy of all documents for yourself just in case, before you hand them to your lawyer. Many of them will be on your computer anyway.

It's very important to select the right lawyer for your case at an early stage. Once you've got it right, stick with your decision, even if things don't go well from time to time. Apart from the financial cost, it does your case no good at all to change lawyers too often.

So how do you get a good lawyer first time when you don't know any lawyers in your town?

A friend might recommend a lawyer to you. Be careful if this happens. Is the recommendation purely on merit, because the lawyer showed great competence in that part of the law with which you're concerned? Or is it a "good buddy" recommendation, made just because the lawyer belongs to the same golf club as your friend? Find out as much as you can about any lawyers recommended to you, whether they specialize in your area of the law, what kind of success rate they've enjoyed recently, and so on.

Whether or not you have any recommended lawyers on your list, take some time and go down to the court where you will be fighting your case. Go on a busy day and sit in the public seating area. There may be several courts all operating at the same time, especially if it's a court covering a city or large metropolitan area. In this case visit each courtroom in turn and listen in on the proceedings. If you have any reliable and astute friends who can help you cover several courtrooms at a time then so much the better.

You'll find that you soon become familiar with the layout of each room, the prosecuting lawyers and the defence lawyers. Look out for good, competent lawyers dealing with cases similar to your own. By studying them, the way they present themselves and their cases, you'll be able to determine if you could work well with them. Because you're a team -- you and your lawyer.

In England many lower courts, civil and criminal, deal with more minor issues - guilty pleas and adjournments, committals to a higher court, and so on -- in the mornings, and reserve the afternoons for trials and full-blown contested hearings. Make sure you listen in on as many contested cases as you can. This will make it more likely that you'll get to know the more successful lawyers. You'll be able to see at first hand how they perform under pressure, how well they can cross-examine and destroy a witness.

Searching out a good lawyer in this manner is vastly preferable to relying on a friend's recommendation. Beware of recommendations made by anyone you speak with at the courthouse. Lawyers' practices of hiring "touts" at court to get some extra business haven't died out. In fact they can do this quite openly in most western countries. Even someone who should know the court's lawyers well, like the court usher, can't necessarily be trusted.

Carrying out this process may take some time, but even if you have to sacrifice some business time or part of your annual paid leave, it will be very well worth it. This method is without doubt the best way to select a good lawyer who will help you win your case in court.

3. Instructing Your Lawyer

There are two skills you should look for in a lawyer/advocate:

1) Expert or specialist knowledge of the law relating to the offence or dispute in question
2) Ability to handle your case in court, that is, to confidently present your case, challenge the opposing lawyer and even the judge if necessary, and, most importantly, to cross-examine your opponent and his witnesses in such a way as to expose any weaknesses in their case and gain the sympathy of the jury.

In many jurisdictions, e.g. the US, one lawyer handles your whole case (though there can be more than one if it is particularly complicated). In others, such as England, you usually have two lawyers, one (a solicitor) to handle it in the lower courts, and a second one (a barrister) who takes over once the case is listed in the higher court (High Court or Crown Court). If the latter system applies to you then at some stage there will be a meeting (or "conference") with the barrister (also known as "counsel") where you will discuss the case with your solicitor and the barrister who will be representing you in court.

In England, while solicitors have had the right of appearance before the Crown Court for many years, it's still more usual to instruct counsel once the case is committed to the higher court.

================

The lawyer-client relationship is what is called "privileged". This means that neither you nor your lawyer can be made to divulge to anyone else, including the police, the prosecution, or any court, what was said between him and you. This rule applies also to communications between you and your barrister, where you have one.

Its purpose is that a citizen may freely consult a lawyer and obtain legal advice free from the fear that in doing so he may be rendering himself liable to prosecution or civil legal proceedings on account of what he says. Similarly, the lawyer is free to give whatever advice he thinks best for his client, without fear of repercussions.

So, for example, if you believe you're guilty of a criminal offence with which you've been charged, you can make whatever admissions about it that you like to your lawyer and he cannot be made to tell anyone else anything of what you said to him. You can establish exactly what possible penalties you may face, what your best strategy is, and so on, without having to worry for the moment about the possible consequences.

But if you tell your lawyer you committed a crime that you've been charged with you cannot then instruct him to defend you on a "not guilty" basis. That would take you into the realms of perjury, a serious criminal offence.

If you're guilty of the offence charged you must give your lawyer an honest account of your actions and leave it to him to represent you in court in such a way as will get you the best result obtainable in the circumstances, i.e. a lenient sentence.

If you don't know for sure whether you're guilty or not, then you have to be honest and frank in your instructions, i.e. your account of what happened. Only in that way can you expect the best advice from your lawyer. There may be a technical defence to the charge that you don't know about. That's why you should never make any admissions to the police until you've received legal advice.

In every case that is being defended the prosecution (in a criminal case) and the plaintiff (in a civil case) have to serve on the accused, or defendant, copies of the evidence on which they intend to rely to prove their case. In England, in criminal cases, this is called "disclosure".In civil cases it is called the "pleadings". The purpose of this procedure is to clarify the issues at stake (in civil proceedings) and to let the accused know exactly what evidence the prosecution intend to produce to the court (in criminal cases).

All this paperwork will be served on your lawyer, who will then arrange to go through it all with you. You will then see exactly what the case is that the prosecution, or plaintiff, has against you. The written account that you first handed your lawyer should prove to be invaluable at this stage.

If your lawyer hasn't already done so, he will "proof" you. What this means is that he will question you, perhaps even "cross-examine" you, just as if you were in court being interrogated by the opposing advocate. Don't be offended or alarmed when this happens. Rather, be pleased that your lawyer is taking your case seriously and displaying some of his advocacy skills. He is testing the truthfulness of your case and how well you will stand up against cross-examination.

Only by testing, or "proofing" you in this way can he be sure that your case is good and that you will make a good witness. If he fails to do this he risks having your case collapse in court for weakness, or unreliability of your evidence. That's not good for his reputation as a lawyer, and of course it's not good for you.

Be prepared for a grilling. This will actually be very beneficial for you and your case. It will expose any weaknesses there may be. Better that you find out what these are at this stage than at court. It's an invaluable preparation for when you are cross-examined for real, later on.

It's vital to establish a good rapport with your lawyer. He has to be able to trust and respect you, and you have to earn that trust. You have to be able to work together as a team, preparing the case or the defence, organizing evidence and witnesses and, if appropriate, instructing a barrister.

Always be punctual at appointments. Dress smart, and have the air of someone who intends to win. Be honest and forthright. Don't hold anything back, even if you think it might not be relevant (let your lawyer decide on that) or helpful. It's better to deal with problems in your case now rather than leave it to when you're being cross-examined by the opposing lawyer.

If you're the defendant, whether it's a civil or a criminal case, go through with your lawyer every single thing that the plaintiff, or prosecution, have to prove. See how many witnesses are giving evidence against you on each point, or head of charge. What do they actually say? Do they all say the same thing (in which case, is there any evidence of collaboration, e.g. similar but unusual expressions used) or are they giving different accounts (in which case their evidence can easily be discredited)?

In fact if you are faced with several witnesses all testifying against you concerning a particular incident that took place, e.g. a fight in a bar, then it can actually be a good thing. Why? Because the more witnesses there are the greater the scope for them to give different versions of what happened. If their accounts substantially differ on a vital point, then their evidence can be destroyed on cross-examination. This will make the plaintiff's, or prosecution, case a mess on that particular point, or charge, and bearing in mind the burden of proof ("beyond reasonable doubt", or "on the balance of probabilities"), it means victory for you may be that much closer.

Give every piece of evidence against you a "forensic" examination. See how it conflicts, as most of it will, with your own evidence. Consider each of the opposing witnesses. Contrast them with your own witnesses. How do they compare in credibility? Do any witnesses, whether for you or against you, have any criminal convictions, particularly of offences involving dishonesty? Your lawyer will make inquiries of his opposite number on the other side on this aspect. Do any witnesses have disabilities, e.g. deafness, poor eyesight, that might affect the reliability of their evidence?

Are any of the opposing witnesses related to, or friendly with, your main protagonist, or anyone allegedly aggrieved by you? Study the opposing witnesses in detail. Get to know all about them - where they live, where they work, where they socialize. Walk or drive along their street and observe their house. Is it cheap or expensive? What sort of vehicles are parked on the driveway? What sort of job do they have, or what business are they in?

Have they been saying anything relating to the case on Facebook or Twitter? You may not have the means to find out everything, but find out as much as you possibly can. There's always going to be something that's of use. Compile a dossier and put all your information in it. When you're through, hand it to your lawyer -- he needs to know all about the other side's witnesses before the court proceedings begin.

Incidentally, you should on no account post anything relating to your case on any social networking site, or indeed any other web site. To do so would cause serious problems to you and your lawyer.

Once again, the secret to winning in court is preparation, preparation, preparation. Plus attention to detail. In the military they say you must know your enemy, and as you're treating the case like a military operation, then it applies to you.

Meet and discuss your findings with your lawyer. He should by then have studied the relevant law intimately, if he's not thoroughly familiar with it already. Go through an abbreviated rehearsal of the court proceedings with him. At home, rehearse giving your evidence. Establish from your lawyer the possible lines of attack that the opposing lawyer may take, and practice dealing with the questions he will put to you, especially on any aspect of your evidence that isn't very strong.

Do the same with your witnesses. Be with them when they are proofed by your lawyer. He should proof them separately, one at a time, and will go through each witness's evidence with them. He will put any likely hostile questions to them to see what their response is. This will help you and your witnesses to become polished and formidable in the witness box. Be careful, though, at all times to avoid putting any pressure on a witness as to what his evidence should be or how he should present it.

Of course, your witnesses can only give evidence of matters within their first hand knowledge. Your lawyer will advise all concerned about this. For example, hearsay evidence is not admissible (e.g. "Fred told me he saw Bill drive into John's gatepost and demolish it.") On no account allow or encourage any witness to lie, or even exaggerate his evidence, no matter how beneficial you may think it would be to your case. This would be perjury, and possibly conspiracy to pervert the course of justice, and is a serious crime. Aside from that, any such manoeuvre is bound to be exposed by the opposing lawyer when he cross-examines the witness, and it would effectively ruin your case.

Finally, make sure you have become familiar with the court that is hearing your case. You probably did this when you were carrying out your research into which lawyer you should instruct. Learn how to address the judge, and which judge is listed to hear your case. Get to know the court clerks and ushers, even if only by sight. Always be polite and friendly, even to lowly court attendants and messengers -- you never know when you may need a favour from them.

When you know which judge is hearing your case, find out as much as you can about him. Ask your lawyer what he thinks of him, what his likes and dislikes are. If he's in any kind of Who's Who, look him up. If he plays golf and so do you then you may be able to throw in a golfing analogy somewhere in your evidence. It may make no difference, of course, but you have nothing to lose in doing this.

It could help make him identify with you more than with the average litigant (or defendant), and help you a lot, as well as being entirely ethical. Remember, in court, you don't necessarily get justice. You get a result, and reading and applying the advice in this section will help you get the result you want.

3. Winning in Court

1. Keeping Your Eye On The Ball

When you arrive at court on the day of the hearing, you'll probably be nervous. If it's a civil action then your opponent will probably be just as nervous.

Dress according to the prevailing standards. Most probably everyone involved in the court administration, as well as the lawyers, will be dressed smartly, in suits with polished shoes, ties for the men, smart blouses for the ladies, and hair properly groomed, so do likewise. You don't want your case prejudiced because the judge or jury can't help contrasting your untidy appearance with the smart dress of your opponent. Remember, it's not just about justice. It's about getting a result.

Arrive punctually. This will be well ahead of the time the actual case is listed. Your lawyer may well want to see you before the start in one of the interview or conference rooms. He will have with him all the documents relevant to your case in your file and in logical order.

Make sure your witnesses, if you have any,

also arrive punctually, and smartly dressed and groomed. Your lawyer or his assistant will show them where they have to wait and give them all the information they need, including when they're likely to be called to give evidence, where refreshments can be obtained, and so on. If you're the defendant, or accused, then they will not be required until the plaintiff, or prosecution, has finished presenting their case. Your lawyer will know how long this is likely to take, so you can allow your witnesses to arrive at that later time, be it later in the day, or a day or two later, or further still, depending on the anticipated length of the case.

Don't allow any of your witnesses to watch or listen to your case before they are called to give evidence, unless your lawyer has said they can. In most cases, in most jurisdictions, this will preclude the witness from giving evidence for you.

During the progress of the case there may well be things that happen or procedures that have to be followed that cause you difficulties and frustration. Most probably this will be no fault of yourself or your lawyer, and if this happens there's nothing that can be done about it. Don't get angry or upset over such matters. You're there to win your case, not overhaul the legal system. Keep your eye on the ball and don't be distracted. This is one of the most important pieces of advice in this Guide.

2. Your Part In The Selection Of The Jury

If a jury is involved in deciding the facts of the case then most probably, depending on which jurisdiction you are in, you are entitled to a say in who is allowed to sit on it. In a criminal case you can object to potential jurors "for cause", i.e. there is some specific reason for you to object, such as you believe he is associated in some way with a prosecution witness. You may be able to object to one or more jurors without disclosing any cause at all. Your lawyer will advise you. You may not need to use this power, but it's useful to know it's there.

When you have entered a plea of "Not Guilty" in a criminal case the jury will be introduced into the court and "sworn in". Each juror in turn will stand up and swear or affirm to give an impartial verdict. This is usually supervised by the court's chief clerk. You have to make sure you're in verbal or visual contact with your lawyer at this stage.

When a juror stands up that you feel would be better not involved in your case, let your lawyer know immediately, and he will make an objection.

The juror will then leave the court and be replaced by another one. Your lawyer will have told you the maximum number of objections, with or without cause, that you're allowed, so be careful not to object unless you really feel you have to.

3. The Case Begins

Unless you are the plaintiff in a civil case then it will be the other side that opens its case first. Your lawyer will take notes from time to time of what each witness says in answering questions put by their own advocate. You don't need to take notes yourself unless the case is complex or you feel it would help you when you come to give evidence.

Whether you take notes or not, you'll naturally be listening intently to the opposition witnesses. If you've done your homework then there shouldn't be any surprises, but don't be afraid to call out to your lawyer to request an adjournment if anything unusual or important arises and you need to consult with him before the case proceeds further.

In a <u>civil case</u>, the plaintiff, or his lawyer, outlines his case to the court and calls his witnesses one by one, usually in order of the importance of their evidence. He examines his first witness by asking questions designed to elicit the evidence he wishes to bring out. Naturally, he only asks questions that the witness can answer from his own first-hand knowledge. He cannot ask "leading questions". He has to let the witness describe what he witnessed in his own words. He cannot ask his witness, for example, "Did you then see Bill punch Fred on the nose?" He would ask, "Can you tell the court what you saw next?"

When he has finished questioning the witness, the defendant's lawyer can ask questions, or "cross-examine" the witness. This time, because it's not his witness, the lawyer can ask "leading questions", e.g. "You were, in fact, still sitting in the car when Fred came out of the house, weren't you?" The idea, of course, is to find inconsistencies and gaps in the witness's evidence and thereby to discredit it in the eyes of the jury.

When the first witness has finished being examined and cross-examined, the second witness takes the stand and the same process takes place, and then the same with the next witness until all the witnesses for the plaintiff, or prosecution, have given their evidence. Exceptionally, a witness can be recalled to be re-examined (and possibly cross-examined further, if appropriate), but only if a matter arises that warrants it.

Then the defendant calls his witnesses. If he is legally represented then he will normally be the first witness. Otherwise he will set out his case and then be liable to cross-examination by the plaintiff's (or prosecution) lawyer. Then he will call his other witnesses to be examined and then cross-examined in the same way.

In a criminal case, the prosecution outlines its case to the jury and then calls its witnesses in order of importance to their case. The same principles apply, generally, as in a civil case, as to examination and cross-examination.

4. Should You Give Evidence?

If you are being prosecuted, or if you are the plaintiff in a civil action, then whilst you could in theory decline to give evidence, especially if you have witnesses to testify on your behalf, it will look decidedly odd, as if you have something to hide or you seek to avoid cross-examination or fear it will destroy your case. The judge or jury (whoever it is who decides whether you win or lose, or are guilty or not guilty) will feel deprived of some of the facts that they ought to have, and that will go against you.

If you're represented by a lawyer then you have to decide between you whether you should give evidence. This will depend on all the factors affecting your particular case, but generally you should give evidence unless there is a compelling reason not to.

5. No Case To Answer?

If you're the accused in a criminal trial, at the close of the prosecution case, it's open for your advocate to submit to the judge that there's no case to answer. This move can only be successful if all the evidence produced by the prosecution is insufficient to support the charge, i.e. even if all their evidence was absolutely true it wouldn't prove that you had committed the offence. The prosecution isn't allowed to cobble together an insufficient case and then rely on you incriminating yourself in cross-examination.

The whole question of "no case to answer" is one that you and your lawyer should have covered early on in the preparation of your case. In most cases it will not be relevant, but occasionally it is, and there have been some high profile cases over the years where a case has been spectacularly thrown out at this stage because there was "no case to answer".

6. Giving Your Evidence

It can be nerve-wracking when you first enter the
witness box to give your evidence. Try not to let this
affect you. Familiarize yourself with the new view
of the courtroom and concentrate on getting your
case across.

You'll be required to either swear on the Bible,
or other religious book of your choice, or to affirm,
if you have no religious beliefs, that the evidence
you give will be "the truth, the whole truth, and
nothing but the truth". Here, as throughout your
evidence, speak loud and clear so everyone in the
court has no difficulty in hearing what you have to
say.

Early in the proceedings you should have
gone through the line of questioning that your
advocate will put you through in court, so the
questions he asks you should be familiar. Be content
to answer each point one at a time. Don't try and
give your whole case in answer to the first question.
Let your advocate guide you from one question to
the next. Give full but succinct replies. Never allow

yourself to stray from answering the question, but give whatever degree of detail is required.

These questions from your own advocate will be friendly, allowing you to give your version of events in your own words.

The most critical part of the case is when you come to be cross-examined by the opposing lawyer. This happens immediately after you have answered your own lawyer's questions. The contrast between the friendly, sympathetic questioning from your own lawyer and the hostile cross-questioning you suddenly find yourself facing from a seasoned professional can be very upsetting and it is vital you and your witnesses prepare for this well in advance.

If you've done your preparation properly then you'll probably know the line of questioning that the opposing lawyer will follow. The important thing to bear in mind is that he is only doing his job -- there's nothing personal. But nevertheless his job is to win the case for his client – and if it's a criminal case then to secure a guilty verdict against you.

A lot of confusion and resentment arises because people who find themselves involved in court proceedings have the idea that everyone is trying to find out the truth -- to seek justice. This is completely untrue. Whilst the judge and jury are only interested in seeking out the truth, the opposing lawyer, and no doubt his witnesses, are only interested in winning the case against you. They're after a result. The lawyer wants another victory to enhance his career, so gradually he'll be able to command higher fees, or be promoted to the bench (i.e. become a judge). Perhaps he's in line for a bonus if he wins this case. And if that means trampling all over your reputation and making you look like a fool or a liar in court, then so be it.

When you're being cross-examined, just remember that the questions being fired at you aren't designed to bring out the truth. They're designed to try and discredit you in the eyes of the jury, or the judge, so that they'll decide the case against you. Realizing this in advance will help you withstand the onslaught and come through it with your case stronger than it was before. Of course, techniques and styles of cross-examination differ, as do skill levels in doing it, but these principles apply to all cross-examinations.

You'll already be familiar with how the opposing lawyer looks by this stage. But probably the only times you've heard him speak are when he has been examining his own witnesses, when naturally he has appeared friendly and pleasant.

Now things are different. Acclimatize yourself as quickly as possible to the new situation, and relax as much as you can in the circumstances. You may sound nervous at first but that will be understandable. You can rest assured that if you have attracted the sympathy of the jury in the honest and straightforward way you have answered your own lawyer's questions, or presented your own case, then they are really feeling for you now.

Be courteous to the opposing lawyer at all times. DO NOT BE PROVOKED. This applies especially if it is part of the other side's case that you are a person of short temper or prone to violent outbursts. What better way to prove their case than for you to have an argument, or to come out with a mouthful of abuse, against the lawyer cross-examining you? No matter how objectionable the opposing lawyer is, or how much he provokes you and belittles you, taunting you with accusations that you may have had to endure for months and know to be untrue, refuse to respond with any kind of abuse.

This will require an immense degree of self control, but you MUST NOT respond. If you do, then you will have fallen into the trap they have set for you, and your case will suffer immeasurably. No matter how satisfying it may be to give him as good as he is handing out, and give him a verbal "smack in the gob", refuse to do so at all costs.

===============

Here are some suggested replies to provocative questions, i.e. questions that suggest you're telling lies, not giving the whole story, covering up, etc.

* "I'm here to tell the truth, and that's what I'm doing."

* "I'm doing my best to give all the facts as I know them to be."

* "You may have that opinion of me, but I doubt that opinion is shared by anyone else."

* "I'm afraid I can't answer that question as I don't have the necessary information."

* "I accept that [name] is not my favourite person, but I don't tell lies under oath about him/her or anyone else."

===============

If you get into an argument with the opposing lawyer you will lose that argument (and probably your case). Remember, he is a skilled professional who wins arguments for his living. And he decides which questions to ask, and he will delight in telling you to "just answer the question" -- lawyer-speak for "just let me distort the facts in my favour -- don't spoil my case with the truth." You're not on a level playing field, SO DON'T GET INTO AN ARGUMENT. Simply repeat your point, if necessary, until he gives up. Don't be drawn into anything other than the facts in dispute. Make sure your witnesses understand everything in this section as well.

Don't allow yourself to be rushed. The opposing lawyer may try this tactic in order to try and confuse you or make you say something you didn't mean to say and that could damage your case. Take your time with each question. Speak in measured tones as far as you can, and always remember that the jury have to be able to hear your replies.

Probably the best way to handle cross-examination is to avoid eye contact as far as possible. Fix your gaze on something close to the lawyer, so it looks to everyone else as if you're looking straight at him. But don't look at his face at all. Concentrate on answering his questions as best you can. Almost certainly you won't be able to answer all of them, and if you can't answer a particular question just say so. If anything, be over-polite. Resist any temptation to give a short, over-simplified reply, or to agree with anything that is almost true, but not completely. This will give him the opportunity to contrast your reply with an earlier statement you may have made and which is at variance with what you've just agreed to, and thereby to accuse you of lying.

If he succeeds he will be able to ask you the question often heard in English courts, "Were you lying then, or are you lying now?" To which, of course, the only answer is, "I'm not lying now and nor was I lying then. I'm just doing my best to answer your questions truthfully."

He'll probably accuse you of lying at some stage, anyway. Don't let this worry you. After all, he's got to accuse you of lying --it's probably central to his case. Keep strictly to the truth, to what you've said all along, even though it means repeating much of what you've said already -- it will reinforce your case in the eyes of the judge and jury.

And remember this - if he comes out with more and more provocation and unpleasantness it's probably a sign of desperation. An experienced lawyer, once he knows he's not getting the desired response from you (or your witness), will cease his questioning once he's put his side of the case to you and you've denied it. Use your cross-examination as a means to win the sympathy of the judge and jury -- you can do this far more effectively in this way than your advocate can in presenting or summing up your case.

7. The Summing Up

Once the witnesses for the prosecution, or plaintiff, and the defence, or defendant, have finished being examined and cross-examined, the summings up commence.

The plaintiff, or prosecution, opens. Their advocate will sum up their case to the court. In a criminal case all advocates address the jury. In a civil case it's normally the judge they address, except in certain cases, e.g. libel.

Next is the defence summing up, where the defence advocate does the same, emphasizing the strong points of the defence and any weak points in the prosecution, or plaintiff's, case, and discussing any important points raised by witnesses, and so on.

Finally, in criminal cases, the judge sums up to the jury. This is an impartial summing up combined with advice, as required, on any complex legal questions that have arisen.

8. The Verdict

Whatever the verdict, accept it for what it is. If your case is good and you've followed the advice in this Guide, then you should get the verdict you want. Don't jump for joy and let out a string of whoopees if it's favourable. Don't express anger or burst into tears if it's against you.

It may not be the end of the episode. If you win you may have to enforce the judgement, if you're the plaintiff in a civil case, or recover your costs if you're the defendant. And if you lost you may in some cases be able to appeal.

If you win, your advocate will ask for an order (if it's allowed) that the other side pay your costs.

If you lose in a criminal prosecution then the judge will deal with sentencing. This may not happen immediately. There may have to be an adjournment for reports or so the judge can consider, in a serious case, what sentence is appropriate.

If this happens, and it is a serious case, the question of bail or being remanded in custody arises. You will have discussed this with your advocate beforehand and he will make any application that may be necessary.

4 - How To Handle Your Home or Business Premises Being Searched

The law gives wide powers to the police and government bodies, e.g the UK's HM Revenue & Customs, to enter and search premises if they have reason to believe there is evidence of crime or tax evasion to be found there. Whilst they have a duty to cause as little damage and disruption as possible, nevertheless in practice there is bound to be rough handling of your property. It can be very upsetting to see complete strangers in your own home or business trampling over your personal or business belongings, not seeming to care if fragile items get broken.

As soon as the search starts you should establish who is in charge of it and consider telephoning your lawyer so he can attend while the search takes place. Insist on seeing and being able to examine the Search Warrant to ensure it has been properly signed and dated and relates to your premises. You can ask for the search to be delayed until your legal adviser arrives, but this request may or may not be granted.

There have been instances of deliberate or

reckless damage being done in house searches and for this reason you'll want to ensure that if this happens to you, you'll be able to prove it and successfully claim compensation for it.

If you are ever in a situation where you believe your home or office premises may be searched, you should obtain evidence of the current state or condition of the property. This means taking a few photographs or a video of the interior of every part of the property that may be affected. With modern smartphones invariably having a camera and camcorder built-in, this shouldn't be difficult or expensive. Make sure you have the date facility on so the date is recorded on the photographs or video.

During the course of such a search, observe as far as possible everything that goes on. If you can, take a video recording of it. The sole purpose of the search is to collect evidence of a crime or tax irregularity. The people making the search have to inform you of the crime or type of tax irregularity that they believe you to have committed. They must restrict their search accordingly, and if they want to search areas or documents that can't contain relevant evidence then you can object.

Focus your photographing or videoing on anything you feel may be of significance later on. If anyone taking part in the search deliberately or recklessly damages or abuses your belongings then you should immediately register a protest or complaint with the officer in charge.

If the search proceeds without any such damage then you should still be vigilant to ensure there is no abuse of your property. If anything of significance is found and removed, make sure you receive a receipt for it. If appropriate, take a picture of it before it is removed, or video it being taken away. Pictures and video that you take before and during the search can be invaluable in proving any damage done or procedures not complied with.

If any items are found that could possibly be used as evidence against you then you may find yourself being asked questions. Remember you have a right of silence. If your legal representative is present then he or she will advise you on that point.

Throughout the search do your best to keep calm and alert. You will probably be observed for any signs of guilt or anxiety. Even for someone completely innocent, it's bound to be a harrowing time, so you can't expect to be the picture of coolness. Nevertheless, keep your self-control as much as possible. Remember that what goes on during the search may well be the subject of evidence given in court later on, so act accordingly.

After the search, you will have to decide whether or not to photograph or video any parts of the area where it took place. This depends on any damage that may have been done or incidents that took place. If you are arrested after the search, try and arrange for someone else to do this if necessary, before the place is tidied up.

---

5 - What To Do If You're Arrested

Note: This Section covers non-terrorist type offences only. Since 2001 anti-terror laws in most western countries have created new offences and procedures relating to those offences. Anti-terror laws and terrorist type offences are outside the scope of this Guide.

Incidentally, be aware that the police cannot detain you against your will unless you have been arrested. I remember attending a police station in London where a client had been detained overnight in a police cell, and was shocked to learn on my arrival that he had not actually been arrested. Obviously I secured his release immediately.

The point is that if you are attending a police station voluntarily you cannot be made to remain there against your will if you haven't been arrested. And the police will only arrest you if they are confident that they have good grounds for doing so.

1. On Being Arrested

Being arrested can be very traumatic, and it won't be easy to keep calm. But that's exactly what you have to do. The police have an obligation to tell you what you are being arrested for, so if they don't tell you then ask them. Get it very clear in your mind exactly what offence it is that you're being arrested for.

If you're arrested in a situation of confusion and disorder, e.g. where there has been an incident involving a large number of people with many being arrested, then it may well be impractical for the police to tell everyone they arrest the precise offence they're being arrested for. But even here they should inform everyone of the reason for their arrest as soon as possible.

No matter how innocent you may be of any wrongdoing, you must conduct yourself in a manner that the judge or jury can feel comfortable with when being asked to find you Not Guilty.

It often happens that, e.g. in a public bar brawl, an innocent bystander gets set upon by the real trouble makers, or somehow caught up in the melee, and the police come along and arrest everyone, including the innocent bystander, who ends up being charged and convicted of something he didn't do.

If you explode with indignation at being wrongly arrested, and use bad language to the police officers involved, you risk damaging your defence, and being lumped together with the real culprits, who are probably also giving the police a hard time.

Don't ever try to resist arrest. It's pointless anyway, and will only make matters worse. That doesn't mean you shouldn't maintain your innocence verbally, and protest that you haven't committed an arrestable offence. But keep your dignity. If you really are innocent, then act innocent.

You'll be subjected to a number of indignities (including having your photograph taken holding a number) as if you were a common criminal, but you mustn't let that affect you. You have to accept from that moment that you are going to be locked up in an uncomfortable cell for several hours and probably interviewed by a couple of unsympathetic police officers who are convinced you are guilty.

2. On Being Interviewed

It is absolutely essential that before the interview takes place you obtain legal advice on your situation. This should preferably be from your own lawyer, though if it is in unsociable hours you may have to be satisfied temporarily with a duty lawyer.

The Duty Lawyer system is usually based on a 24 hour rota, so no matter what time of day or night it may be there should always be a lawyer available to help you.

Of course, you don't have to engage that lawyer for the case, in the event that you are charged. In most cases the duty lawyer simply advises the arrested person on how to handle the interview, gives preliminary legal advice, and maybe applies for bail, leaving the client to instruct his regular lawyer later on.

The duty lawyer should have enough knowledge and experience to handle matters for you until such time as your own lawyer or one of your choosing is available. Nevertheless, it is preferable by far to consult with your own lawyer before agreeing to be interviewed by the police.

The reason is that in some countries in recent years the right of silence has been compromised. That's certainly the case in the United Kingdom. Previously it was possible to refuse to answer any questions at the police station and then later to defend the case on whatever basis you chose. Now, you have to disclose at the interview any facts on which you intend to rely in your defence or which it would have been reasonable for you to mention at the time.

Unless you know the law relating to this in your country it's best to take advice from a lawyer.

================

A good example where the right of silence is not absolute is where there is an alibi. This can arise where someone is arrested for an offence that took place some time earlier. If his defence is that he was elsewhere at the time of the offence, and therefore he couldn't possibly have committed it, then he has (in addition to disclosing this fact at interview) to give details in his Defence Statement (given later on), including details of witnesses who can corroborate his alibi. This is so the prosecution can check out the alibi before the case comes to court, and to inhibit a guilty person who attempts to "manufacture" an alibi.

===============

There are also other restrictions on the right of silence in certain circumstances, and because of these complications you should take legal advice before the interview commences.

The next rule is to keep calm. I once had to attend a police station interview of a client -- a businessman -- who had just been arrested on a charge of falsifying a cheque. Several thousands of pounds were involved and although he had no previous convictions if he were to have been found guilty he could have been sent to prison for at least a year, and his business would have been ruined.

I remember that interview above all the other hundreds of such interviews I sat in on because the client was absolutely calm, and in full control. He appeared to be totally unconcerned at the seriousness of the situation. Cold as ice, he was so self-assured that he completely un-nerved the two police officers who interviewed him. He was released without charge within a couple of hours.

The question is -- apart from disclosing facts that you have to disclose in order to be able to rely on them later -- do you answer questions or not?

This is where the right legal advice is absolutely essential. Each case must be considered on its own merits, but the general rule must be that you should not answer any further questions. Of course there may be exceptions to this rule, but generally answering questions is not to your advantage, and can only result in a case being built against you.

Besides, when it's so soon after what may well have been a traumatic event, such as a bar room brawl or a motor accident, and you're still in a state of shock at having been arrested, having had to tell your spouse or partner by phone that you've been arrested, and having been locked up in a horrible cell for a few hours and treated like a criminal, it's not exactly the right time to present a well-thought out, mature and lucid defence to the allegations against you.

However truthful you are, in your answers to dozens of questions at the police station, and later on at court in your answers to dozens of questions from the prosecution lawyer, there are bound to be some discrepancies. This will delight the prosecution lawyer, who will make as much capital out of it as he possibly can in attempting to show you up as a liar, and he may well ask (as they often do), "Were you lying then, or are you lying now?"

If that happens, your case will have been severely, perhaps fatally, damaged. For that reason alone, don't answer any questions at the police station (apart from divulging any facts, as stated above, that you have to disclose) unless your lawyer advises that it is absolutely in order to do so in your particular circumstances.

Of course, just because you decide not to answer questions doesn't stop the police from asking them. They'll try and trick you into answering a few by following on from your name and address (which, of course, you'll give) with questions about the incident as if those questions were on an equal footing with confirmation of your name and address. Don't fall for it. Name and address only.

They will express surprise and dismay, even bewilderment, at your refusal to answer questions. They will make you feel awkward and to blame, just as if you were guilty of the offence they want to charge you with. They will tell you the whole matter can be cleared up quickly and you can go home if only you will "co-operate" and answer a few questions.

Explain politely that it has nothing to do with "co-operation", but that you would prefer not to answer questions unless and until you have to give evidence in court. If they ask further questions, you can reply "No comment" to each one.

They may, if you are arrested with others, tell you that one of them has made a statement putting all the blame on you. Would you therefore not like to give your side of the story? Do not fall for that one.

They may even "bang you up" again (slam the cell door really hard so, psychologically, it seems to have been shut for good) to try and break your resolve not to answer questions.

Stick it out. They will have to either charge you or release you within a relatively short time. This varies according to the jurisdiction and the offence for which you have been arrested.

Many people have been wrongly convicted because they gave so much information to the police after their arrest, in the hope of just getting out of that awful place, that inevitably some of it contradicted what they said later on in court.

If you can just control your fear and be patient then your rewards are

(a) you have a much higher chance of being released without charge

(b) even if you are charged, you and your lawyer can prepare your defence in court without being bound or compromised by what you said at the police station, thereby vastly increasing your chances of acquittal.

===============

While you're being kept in custody you may be asked to undergo certain procedures, such as an identity parade (see *Section 6*), being photographed, and even strip searched if appropriate and having intimate body samples taken.

Your rights in these cases are governed by the law in your own country, and because of that, and the fact that such law is changed and amended frequently, I have not covered such matters (apart from identity parades, and then only in general terms). It's far better for you to seek legal advice from a lawyer experienced in criminal procedure.

6 - How To Handle an Identity Parade

1. The Basics

In the UK the rules as to identity parades are regularly amended, and that's probably the case in most jurisdictions. What follows here is generalized advice. You are advised to get more specialized advice relating to your own area. You could start by searching for 'identity parade procedure [your state/country]' in Google, and make sure any pages you read relate to where you live.

In the UK at the present time the relevant document issued under the *Police and Criminal Evidence Act 1984* is *The Code of Practice for the Identification of Persons by Police Officers*.

We all know what an identity parade (or ID parade) is. The police love it when the witness (victim of crime) comes in, looks at the dozen or so people, all looking fairly similar, lined up and unhesitatingly picks out their suspect as being the villain they saw commit a crime, or who robbed or assaulted them, etc.

If you're under arrest and being questioned in connection with a crime and the police tell you they want you to take part in an ID parade, you have to agree. Whilst you could refuse in theory -- no-one (not even the police) can force you to against your will -- you would be foolish to decline and have to deal with the obvious insinuations of guilt later on.

2. What Happens?

In England, and probably most other western countries, what normally happens is that you arrive at a predetermined time, normally at the police station where the case is being handled, and stand in line with a number of other people that the police have usually collected together off the street, to make 10 or 12 in total. The witness(es) are then led in one at a time accompanied by a police officer and invited to identify the villain by touching him. After confirming their selection they're led away.

Your objective, of course, is to avoid being identified by any of the witnesses. Your preparation for this should start well beforehand. Don't assume, just because you know it wasn't you, that you won't be picked out. As soon as you're asked to attend an ID parade, arrange to see a local criminal lawyer who is well-experienced in ID parades. I cover the subject of selecting a lawyer in detail in the main part of this Guide, but for now I want you to realize the importance of having a confident, knowledgeable and competent lawyer with you at this crucial juncture.

3. You and Your Lawyer

It may be that the police are in a hurry to hold the parade, and pressure you to agree a time before you've had a chance to seek legal advice. Resist this at all costs. Explain politely that you're getting as early an appointment as possible with your lawyer and that it will have to take place after that.

Make absolutely sure that the lawyer you consult has considerable expertise in that part of the criminal law that now affects you, AND that he is the person who will attend the ID parade with you. Ask how many ID parades he has attended in the last couple of years, and what sort of success rate he has obtained. Go over the procedure and arrange to meet up with him at the time and place agreed with the police.

If you have good grounds to think that the

lawyer doesn't have much experience with ID parades or commitment to winning your case then don't be afraid to insist on having another lawyer who does have such qualifications. And if that means postponing the ID parade then so be it.

Don't be fobbed off with a junior clerk or trainee who is still gathering experience. Let them learn on someone else. Many law firms will send such a junior employee if you let them, especially if they consider you're guilty anyway and that the result is a foregone conclusion, or they just don't understand the significance of an ID parade.

Someone with limited experience or who is some kind of junior just won't carry the clout required to stand up to the police if they try to cut corners and conduct the proceedings in a wrongful or prejudicial manner.

Now just because you're instructing your lawyer in connection with the ID parade, it doesn't mean that you have to retain his services for the whole case. Make it clear at the outset that you're using his services just for the ID parade at this stage and that you've thought no further than that. (After all, sometimes the police will drop the case altogether if the witnesses fail to select their suspect.) Be careful not to cause offence or appear condescending. If you put it straightforwardly any decent lawyer (there are some about!) will understand you and do his utmost to add another success to his record at your ID parade.

Make sure you and your lawyer arrive in good time, and separately (to avoid the risk of any of the witnesses seeing you with a (usually) easily recognizable lawyer and thereby jumping to the conclusion that you are the person they have to pick out, before the ID parade has even begun!) In most places the police go to great lengths to comply with the law relating to ID parades, to prevent the witnesses from seeing any of the participants before the parade begins, e.g. using separate entrances and waiting rooms.

4. What To Watch Out For

You will be introduced into the room where the parade is to take place. The other participants will probably already be there. Take a good look at them one by one. Remember, they have all been selected and vetted by the police.

Now the police do have to abide by certain rules when organizing an ID parade. They have to select participants who bear a reasonable resemblance to you. But there is inevitably a degree of uncertainty, where interpretations may differ. So it may be that one or two of the participants bear little resemblance to you in any way.

You should be able to leave all the work to your lawyer here. Be willing to let him intervene as necessary on your behalf. Whilst it's impractical to expect the police to produce a dozen lookalikes, at the same time none of them should be so different in appearance, age or demeanour that they bear no resemblance at all to you.

Be aware of any strong body smells, whether natural or artificial, e.g. alcohol on the breath, or after-shave lotion, that would rule out that person.

If you've been kept in custody you're likely to be looking the worse for it. But you can still shave and make yourself smart (if that's how you usually are), and suitable clothes will have to be made available for you. Have friends or family attend with a selection of your usual clothes, if possible. Avoid having the air of someone who's been locked up for a day or two, if that applies to you.

If you are a smart looking person then you want all participants looking smart. If you are scruffy then everyone should be scruffy. Don't be afraid to object to any participant who is so distinctly unlike you that any comparison is just silly. You'd be surprised at what the police try and get away with at times, just to make up the numbers.

5. Standing in Line

I've been present at parades where I've been asked to agree a smaller number of participants than the required minimum -- 7 or 8 instead of 12 -- because the police just can't produce enough volunteers who sufficiently resemble their subject. Never agree to this.

When everyone is ready you will be asked to take your place in the line-up. Your lawyer should have helped supervise where everyone stands. You're entitled, as the suspect, to determine where not only you yourself stand but where others on the line-up stand as well. So where is best?

There's no straightforward answer to this. The witness will quite probably expect to find the suspect right in the middle of the line-up, so it may be best to stand one or two places from one end or the other. My advice has always been based on standing my client next to the participant who most resembles him in facial features. If they are of similar height to you then that's even better. Whilst everyone should be more or less the same height as you, there will invariably be some taller and some shorter than you, unless you are exceptionally tall or short. This won't matter much unless the height of the suspect is a prime identifying factor. The objective is that if the witness is unsure before he enters the room then he'll be even more uncertain when looking at two similarly looking individuals standing next to each other.

It'll be quite nerve-wracking for you when you're standing in line with the witness being led by a police officer, looking intently at each person in turn. The others probably won't be nervous at all, because the outcome doesn't matter to them. This can show up in facial expressions and is sometimes the deciding factor in a witness making an identification (whether correct or not). Nervousness can trigger a kind of psychological communication to the witness and can be interpreted as guilt.

Avoid this as best you can. Try and mimic the facial expression of the person next to you, who you have selected as looking most like you. Quite probably this will be one of boredom, interspersed with flashes of brief interest when something happens, such as the witness entering the room.

The police officer supervising will probably tell all participants to simply look straight ahead when it's their turn to be scrutinized. Do this with the same kind of bored expression that most of the others will have, just as if you, too, had been pulled off the street to give up some of your time to make up the numbers at an ID parade, and you, too, are looking forward to getting back to whatever you were doing before, a little the richer as a reward for your time. Participants may be asked to turn around, make various movements, etc, in which case when it's your turn act as if you are bored or a little lethargic.

6. If an Identification is Made

Don't display any emotion, even when an identification is made, whether of you or someone else. Remember, the witness can always change his mind before he leaves the room (though it would weaken the identification for the prosecution). So even if you are picked out, don't give anything away. Don't flicker your eyes. Give the overall impression of boredom at all times - with just the hint of a surprise if you are actually selected.

If there is more than one witness to make an identification then you should be free to change your position in the line-up, and that of any other person in it. If the first witness fails to identify you then it may be best not to change anything. If you are identified then try changing the order of the line-up, but still position yourself next to the same person, looking most like you.

If you're picked out in a way which suggests the identifier is not sure, it may be that unless this is corroborated by at least one other witness positively identifying you then this one act of identifying you may not be relied on or even referred to by the prosecution in their case against you.

When it's over, there will be a delay in leaving, while the witness(es) are seen on their way. If you've been picked out by one or more witnesses then it's likely you'll be charged, whether straight away or later on. If you haven't been picked then the chances increase that you'll never be charged. But even if you have been identified as the culprit, the battle's far from lost. It's only just begun.

7 - Representing Yourself Without a Lawyer

If you are handling your case without a lawyer then, whether you're the plaintiff, the defendant, or the accused in a criminal case, you have to be aware of certain rules that apply generally in all common law jurisdictions, when evidence is being given in court. If you follow the following rules you should give yourself and your case the best chance of success.

Before you call your witnesses you should give a brief outline of your case, e.g.

> *"Your Honour [or however you address the judge in your court], my case is that the accident in question was no fault of mine, but was caused by the excessive speed and lack of care in the plaintiff's driving. I shall also call evidence to support my case that I was driving carefully and at a proper speed, and at no time strayed onto the wrong side of the road. I have three witnesses, not including myself."*

You should then give your own evidence. When you represent yourself, in most jurisdictions you have to give sworn evidence. Obviously you won't be asking yourself questions and then answering them, but you should give a clear, succinct account of the events as you experienced them. Remember, no hearsay evidence. Only cover what you can actually vouch for first hand.

Don't refer to the evidence you expect any of your witnesses to give. Cover all the facts as you maintain them to be. You can't later refer to anything in your case if you or one of your witnesses haven't raised it at this stage. When you've finished, you'll be cross-examined by the opposing lawyer (see below).

As mentioned before in this Guide, you cannot ask leading questions of your own witnesses. Allow them to give their evidence in their own words. However, that doesn't mean you can't introduce matters that aren't in dispute, to save time, e.g. "At around 8.00pm on 18th July, were you in the bar of Central Hotel on Main Street?"

Once you've established all the relevant things that aren't in dispute and you're dealing with things that are, you have to ask <u>short,</u> <u>limited</u> questions, that don't invite a particular kind of answer, and that can be answered briefly. Don't ask, "Did Bill look angry?" Ask, "How did Bill look?" Don't ask, "Did the Ford Estate come out of Side Street into Main Street without stopping and collide with my car?"

Ask, "Did you see the Ford Estate in Side Street?" When the answer is "Yes", ask, "Can you please tell the court what you then saw the Ford Estate do?", and if necessary, "Did the Ford Estate stop at the junction of Side Street with Main Street?"

Don't try and present your case when asking questions (a common mistake among litigants in person). You do that later, in the summing up, and sometimes briefly when you open your case before calling your first witness, as mentioned above.

Keep your witness fully under your control. Don't allow him to ramble on, as many would do if given the chance. Make it clear that you just want one reply on each specific question you ask. This is where preparation, preparation, and yet more preparation pays golden dividends.

By rehearsing several times with your witnesses you can accustom them to answering one point at a time and not deviating from the point or going on to give hearsay evidence, which is not admissible. There's nothing worse than having the judge intervene (and perhaps take over the questioning of your witness, as some will if given the chance) to control your witness, and force him to keep to the questions asked.

If you follow this rule then you'll present a polished, professional performance and thereby impress the judge and jury. This may help ensure that, if there's any doubt about the case, it's resolved in your favour.

Judges are obliged to give assistance where necessary, in an impartial way, to litigants in person who obviously need it to present their case properly. However, this wastes time and saps the patience of most judges, so if you can save your judge the trouble then he'll appreciate it. All part of the strategy of getting him on your side.

================

Summing Up Your Case

The summing up is one of the more difficult things that you'll have to do if you represent yourself. Even lawyers often turn in a poor performance here.

The best advice I can give here is to be brief. That's not to say necessarily that the whole summing up exercise is not to last long - it all depends on the complexity of the case and how many points of contention there are.

But on each point, summarize your case and say why that should be accepted as the truth. Draw the attention of the judge or jury to all the weaknesses of the opposition case on that point.

Summarize the evidence given by your witnesses and explain why each of your witnesses can be believed, that they're honest and have given a true account of the facts they witnessed. Mention any witnesses for the other side who have inconsistencies in their evidence, or who were in a poor position to observe events adequately, and so on.

In short, highlight the strengths of your case and why it should be accepted, and stress the weaknesses or unreliability of your opponent's case and his witnesses.

If appropriate, remind the judge and jury, if you are the defendant or accused, that the plaintiff or prosecution has to prove his/their case, and of the burden of proof -- "beyond reasonable doubt" or "on the balance of probabilities". If you're the plaintiff, ask the tribunal or court to accept that you've proved your case satisfactorily and that the defendant has failed to rebut any part of your case.

That's it. I've seen many cases lost because the

lawyer droned on with no obvious purpose and only succeeded in boring the jury or lay justices. I've also seen litigants in person lose their case largely because they had no idea what a summing up was, and failed to underline the strengths of their case and the weaknesses of their opponent's.

If you follow the advice set out in this Guide you should avoid these pitfalls and give yourself the best possible chance of winning your case in court.

8 - How To Pursue and Contest Custody and Maintenance Claims

I'm only going to cover custody and maintenance claims briefly, because what I've said in the previous sections applies, suitably adapted, here, and in any event you'll almost certainly need specialist legal advice from a local lawyer.

Again, the advice I give here is NOT legal advice, but guidance on how to conduct yourself in order to obtain the best result you can in the circumstances.

It's very rare now to have a contested divorce case. The law in most, if not all, western countries allows a divorce, even with a lack of consent, after a certain period of time has elapsed since the parties separated. In the UK this period is five years.

In most cases both sides want a divorce, or at least recognize that the marriage is effectively over and so there's no point in contesting a divorce. For that reason the only matters liable to be contested are custody of the children, if any, division of property, and maintenance either of a spouse or the children, or both.

Division of property is in most cases agreed and is in any event outside the scope of this Guide. Child custody and maintenance issues are also not covered here in detail because the law differs widely from one jurisdiction to another.

However, what I will say is this. If you are pursuing or contesting an application for child custody or for maintenance for yourself or your children, then it's important to make your case sound as reasonable as possible in the circumstances.

It's easy to get emotional where your own children are concerned, so keeping your temper and maintaining your composure, as described in *Section 3 -- Winning In Court*, is vitally important. Of equal importance here is finding a good lawyer to represent you as described in *Section 2 -- Preparing To Win*.

In the UK and probably in most, if not all, other western jurisdictions, the welfare of the children is paramount. If your claim for custody of the children, for example, is seen not to be in their best interests then it will fail.

In recent times it has become quite common for custody of the children to be awarded to both parents jointly. Obviously they can only live with one parent, given that the two parents have separated, but important decisions such as education and upbringing have to be made jointly, and reasonable access granted to the parent they are not living with.

When presenting your case or giving evidence on any matter affecting your children, always remember that they are the court's first and foremost consideration. If you appear to be putting your own interests before those of the children then it will go down very badly with the court. So act at all times with the interests of your children at heart. This shouldn't need to be said, but it does sometimes happen that one or other parent comes across as being selfish and treating the children as a bargaining point against the other parent.

This accusation may be put to you by the other side, so be prepared. If you manage to impress the judge with your integrity and unselfishness, and your concern for your children where applicable, then you should get the best result possible in the circumstances.

Appendix - How To Recover Money Owing To You (Including Draft Letters)

This section is for people who are owed money for goods or services supplied, typically in the course of a business but not necessarily so.

How do you start? How do you tell the other party that you can't wait any longer for the money owed and that if they don't pay now then you'll sue them in court?

Invariably you have to send the debtor a <u>Letter Before Action</u>. This is a letter to the debtor requesting payment of the money owed by a certain date (usually 7 - 14 days from the date of the letter) failing which you'll issue court proceedings to recover it.

You should always write a letter before action. If you are referring to a contract then the contract may require it anyway. Set out concisely what your claim is for, the amount you are demanding and the time by which the debtor must pay it.

There are a number of sample letters set out in this Appendix. You will probably be able to use or adapt one of these. Keep the letter short and always be prepared to actually carry out the threat of court proceedings. Even though the letter may not result in payment, you can at least confirm to the court later on that you sent the debtor a formal demand for payment. This is invariably a requirement before proceedings are commenced.

If you have personal knowledge of the defendant you will know if you can tone down the letter or offer to accept payment by installments. If you do send a "softer" letter and it brings no response then send the standard letter referring to the earlier letter. Keep copies of all letters sent, and notes of all telephone conversations and personal visits from or to the debtor.

One further note here. When I was writing the first edition of this Guide cheques were still widely used. Now, just a few years later, cheques are a thing of the past. Hardly anyone uses them. Direct transfer by debit or credit card is the norm. Nevertheless, I have retained all references to cheques to cover such people as do still use them.

Most businesses have an online card payment facility, and if that is you then you will no doubt substitute a request to pay in that manner rather than by cheque. Where I have referred to an option to send post-dated cheques, that can be replaced by a request to pay immediately online but with the date of each installment being set into the future, e.g. the last day of each month until all installments are paid.

Finally, bear in mind that the letter you write may well be produced to the court at some stage, so don't put anything abusive or threatening in it, and don't say or imply that non-payment is a crime or a matter for the police, because it isn't. Date all letters and keep copies for yourself.

Example Letters Before Action

1. Dishonoured cheque

Dear Sir,

I write in connection with the cheque dated (date) drawn on (bank) for £/$___ in favour of myself. This cheque has been returned unpaid by your bank. I am now presenting it again. If it is not paid then I shall have no alternative but to issue proceedings for the recovery of this amount plus interest without further notice. This will involve me in additional costs which I shall seek to recover directly from you.

I hope it won't be necessary for me to do this. You

may still settle the amount in cash or a bank draft by no later than (date).

Yours,

==================

2. Money for goods supplied and/or services rendered

(i)

Dear Sir,

I refer to my account/invoice number _____ in the sum of £/$_____ submitted on (date). Although I have telephoned and/or written to you requesting payment this account remains unpaid.

Unless you pay in full or make a realistic proposal for payment by (date) I shall have no alternative but to issue proceedings against you for the full amount due (plus interest) without further notice.

This will involve me in additional costs which I shall claim from you. Please make your cheque payable to (your name or business name) and send it to the address at the top of this letter.

Yours,

(ii)

Dear Sir,

I refer to my account/invoice number _____ in
the sum of £/$_____ submitted on (date). You may
recall having received a reminder/telephone call
from me recently when I asked you to pay this sum
as soon as possible.

I understand you are experiencing financial
difficulties at present and intend to clear this matter
up as soon as you can. While I have no wish to make
matters worse for you, I must ask for some definite
proposals for payment and that these are received by
me no later than (date). I might add that such
proposals would be most favourably received if
accompanied by post-dated cheques for the total
amount due.

I look forward to your early reply.

Yours,

Note: The second version should only be sent to a

debtor you know to be genuinely in financial difficulties. Maybe someone you know well and who is normally a good payer. The number of days you allow for payment will depend on the circumstances, but will normally be 10 to 14 days from the date you send the letter. If you receive no reply, send another letter in the terms of the first version and referring to your earlier letter having brought no response.

================

3. Money lent and not repaid

Dear Sir,

I refer to the sum of £/$_____ borrowed by you from me on (date) under the terms of a written/oral agreement made between us on (date of agreement). Repayment was to have been made by you on (date).

As you know, this amount has not yet been repaid in full/at all. I therefore have to inform you that unless you pay the sum of £/$_____ to me by no later than (date) I shall have to issue recovery proceedings without further notice.

This will involve me in additional costs which I shall seek to recover from you.

Yours,

Note: If the debtor has repaid with a cheque that has been dishonoured then consider using example letter # 1 above. If part of the loan has been repaid then you will demand the outstanding balance. If the loan agreement stipulates repayment by installments then defaulting on one installment invariably renders the whole debt immediately due and payable.

==============

4. Letter demanding the return of money paid for goods or services that are unsatisfactory

Dear Sir.

I refer to (description of goods) that I purchased from you/your company on (date). This item is faulty in that (describe defects).

=== or ===

I refer to the (description of services performed) carried out by you/your workmen on (date). This work is defective in that (describe faults with work done, etc.).

In view of this/these defect(s), I am asking for the

return of the purchase price/deposit/agreed fee of £/$_____ paid to you. [The (description of the goods) will then be immediately returned to you in the same condition it was in when I took possession of it/them.] Please repay this amount to me by no later than (date), failing which I shall commence court proceedings.

Yours,

Note: This is a general form of wording and you will probably have to amend it to suit the circumstances.

=================

5. Accident Damage Letters

(i) Letter to the third party responsible for inflicting damage on your vehicle in a road accident

Dear Sir,

Road Accident - (date)

I refer to the above road accident involving your vehicle (make/model of vehicle and registration number) and my (make/model of vehicle and registration number). I am holding you responsible for causing this accident. Please confirm within the next seven days, i.e. by no later than (date), that you accept liability and that you have lodged a claim with your insurers. [Please also let me have full details of your insurance, including the name and address of your insurers, policy number and claim reference if known.]

Yours,

Note: This is a general form of wording that may have to be adapted to suit your case. You should have obtained details of the other side's insurance at the time of the accident, but sometimes this is not possible. If you or your passengers suffered injury from the accident then you should obtain legal advice and leave the letter-writing to your lawyer. This letter is designed to obtain an admission of liability. The amount of damages can then probably be negotiated.

(ii) Letter to third party's insurers requesting an admission of liability

Dear Sirs,

Your Insured: (Name), Policy No. _____

You should have received details from your above-named insured concerning a road accident that occurred at approximately (time) on (date) at (place) in which his vehicle (make/model and registration number) was in collision with my vehicle (make/model and registration number).

As a result my vehicle suffered the following damage:

(list)

Please note there may be further damage that comes to light when a more thorough inspection of my vehicle takes place.

I am holding your insured responsible for this accident. Would you please confirm liability is accepted by you. I shall then let you have a detailed estimate.

Yours,

==================

What if the debtor offers to pay by installments?

You have to decide quickly whether to accept or reject the offer. If you reject it the debtor could later make the same offer to the court, and the court would only reject it if he could obviously afford to make a better offer.

Bear in mind the debtor may be playing for time. But if you're satisfied it's a genuine offer then reply accepting it provided the first installment is paid immediately, and the balance also sent to you by way of post dated cheques(or post-dated bank transfers if you have that facility available). If there is an agreement allowing you to claim interest in these circumstances then quote the clause concerned and claim the interest.

If the debtor fails to meet any of these requirements then you are justified in issuing proceedings for immediate payment of the full amount due.

It may be that you need more information about the debtor's financial circumstances before you can decide whether to accept his offer. Write him a letter along the lines of the example letter set out below, requesting information about his income and fixed outgoings, savings and debts, etc. If he doesn't reply or give you this information then you're justified in starting court proceedings.

If you do accept payment by installments make sure you obtain post dated cheques (or the digital alternative). Remember to still keep your written notes, or diary of events, so that if you have to give evidence in court later on, where, e.g., a cheque or online payment has been countermanded, you have all relevant facts easily to hand. And, of course, keep copies of all correspondence sent, as well as the originals of received correspondence.

=================

6. Letter to the debtor requesting financial information

Dear Sir,

I refer to your letter dated (date) containing your offer to pay the amount you owe me by [insert number] installments. So that I may make an informed decision, please let me have the following information within the next [seven] days. If you need more time please write and request this, giving your reasons.

Value of house
Value of car or other vehicle
Value of savings
Value of all other assets (furniture, jewellery, etc.)

Amount of mortgage on house
Amount (if any) owing on car or other vehicle

Other debts (if any)

Salary or income from business, (net, per month)
Spouse's net income per month
Rental income from property (if any) per month
State benefits
Any other income

Mortgage or rent payments
Car loan payments
Other debt repayments
Food and household expenses
Gas
Electricity
Telephone/Broadband
Travel including petrol/diesel
Car servicing
Home insurance
Life assurance
TV/Satellite
HP and Credit Sale

(etc., etc.)

I await hearing from you as soon as possible so as to prevent the issue of court proceedings.

Yours,

=================

Commencing Proceedings

If you don't have a satisfactory response two or three days after your deadline has expired (to allow for postal delays, public holidays, etc.) then commence proceedings in the appropriate civil court. The procedure for this varies from one jurisdiction to another and is outside the scope of this Guide. However, the following advice will apply wherever you are.

Review your case. If the debtor denies or puts you to strict proof of everything, you have to produce evidence in support of your claim. Often this will be a simple invoice or the statement of a witness, but there may be expert evidence you need to produce, such as a report from a motor engineer setting out the damage to your vehicle. Arrange for this as soon as it is evident that your claim is going to be defended.

To what standard do you have to prove your case? In civil cases it is normally on the "balance of probabilities", which is less onerous than in criminal cases, where the prosecution have to prove their case "beyond reasonable doubt".

After you've reviewed your case, turn to your dossier on the debtor. If you obtained a judgement, could he pay? Do you have all the details you need -- his full name, address, any business name used, and so on? Are there any bankruptcy or insolvency proceedings currently against him? How long has he lived at his address? Does he own it, or is it rented or in someone else's name? What other debts does he have and are there any default proceedings?

Once you decide to proceed, pursue the case vigorously. Observe time limits scrupulously, as most courts are very strict on this. Don't let your case drift. If you are in business, assign the case to a reliable employee to leave you free to get on with other things.

In Closing

There you have it. Winning in court isn't such a mountain to climb, after all.

Some of the most satisfying moments of my career in the law have been in court watching and listening as one or other of my clients, thoroughly prepared, withstood a gruelling cross examination from the opposing lawyer and came through comparatively unscathed to win the case. Now, if it comes to it, you can do the same. Because you now know how to

- keep a journal recording all relevant developments,
- examine any evidence brought against you dispassionately and logically,
- collect and safeguard the evidence you need to win your case,
- handle yourself at an ID Parade,
- seek out the best legal representation (unless you wish to represent yourself, in which case you know how to best do that as well),
- deal with a police search of your home or office premises,
- prevail in a savage cross-examination from a seasoned professional,

- ensure your witnesses don't let you down in the witness box,
- conduct yourself in court to win the respect of the judge and jury, so if there's the slightest doubt it will be resolved in your favour,
- and more.

I hope you've enjoyed reading this Guide as much as I've enjoyed writing it.

If you feel able, please leave a review and rating on Amazon at this link: https://bklnk.com/B009WUSV0U (that will take you to the Amazon page for this book for your country, whichever country you live in).

About The Author

I was born in Bromley, near London, UK, and I've lived and worked in London, Essex, Cambridge, Norfolk and Leicestershire, which is in the East Midlands region of England.

I wanted to be a Solicitor ever since I was about twelve. I bought a paperback book with a picture on the front cover of a solicitor on the steps of his law office saying goodbye to a lady client, and I could just see myself doing the same kind of thing. I focused the rest of my education on obtaining at least the minimum qualifications to obtain entry to Law School.

In 1973 I qualified as a Solicitor of the Supreme Court of England and Wales and practised for 20 years, mostly as a sole practitioner in my own law practice. Fitting in with the mainstream wasn't for me, somehow. I was much happier working on my own. I could always obtain Counsel's Opinion (advice from a specialist barrister) when required.

I had a rollercoaster of a ride for around fifteen years, starting with just one secretary/telephonist (no computers in those days) and eventually employing a staff of seven. When the lease came to an end the landlords wanted a 400 per cent increase in the rent.

I took a deep breath and moved out of town. All right for residential conveyancing, but not exactly the best place for criminal advocacy. Then I had a doctor's warning about stress and blood pressure, followed by an arson attack that targeted all my client files (the perpetrator(s) was/were never caught). I decided to leave private practice, and some years later I ceased law practice completely, restricting myself to writing legal articles from time to time for the legal press, including, on one occasion, the leader for the prestigious *Law Society Gazette*.

During my practising years I acted for hundreds of clients and appeared in dozens of courts, from magistrates and juvenile courts to the Crown Court.

I've attended at police stations at nearly all times of the day and night to advise on all kinds of criminal law to clients both innocent and guilty, and I've made more bail applications than I can remember. Often as the Duty Solicitor, on call for 24 hours at a time, I had to advise at a moment's notice, and race from one police station to another (as did all duty solicitors). But, hey – I loved it.

And I did meet my wife that way – she came in to see me one day out of the blue for a divorce (not from me, you fool, from her previous husband – LOL). Over 36 years later I have no regrets and she's never told me she has any either – LOL.

Back to the serious stuff. In the civil courts, I've handled hundreds of cases for both plaintiff and defendant. In the criminal courts even more. And as for matrimonials….

In all that time I studied what were the most successful tactics to use in a large number of different situations where my clients found themselves caught up in legal proceedings, or the threat of them. This Guide is the result.

For more about me (you're really sure?), visit my Amazon Author's page at https://urlpeg.com/kindle

27th May 2022